Coloring and Activity Book

SPRINGTIME ADVENTURES™

KAPPA Books

Visit us at www.kappapublishing.com/kappabooks

IT'S SPRINGTIME AND IT'S TIME FOR THE ANNUAL ANIMAL EASTER PICNIC.

FILL IN THE BLANKS ON THE SIGN.

ROBIN JUST RETURNED FROM THE SOUTH.

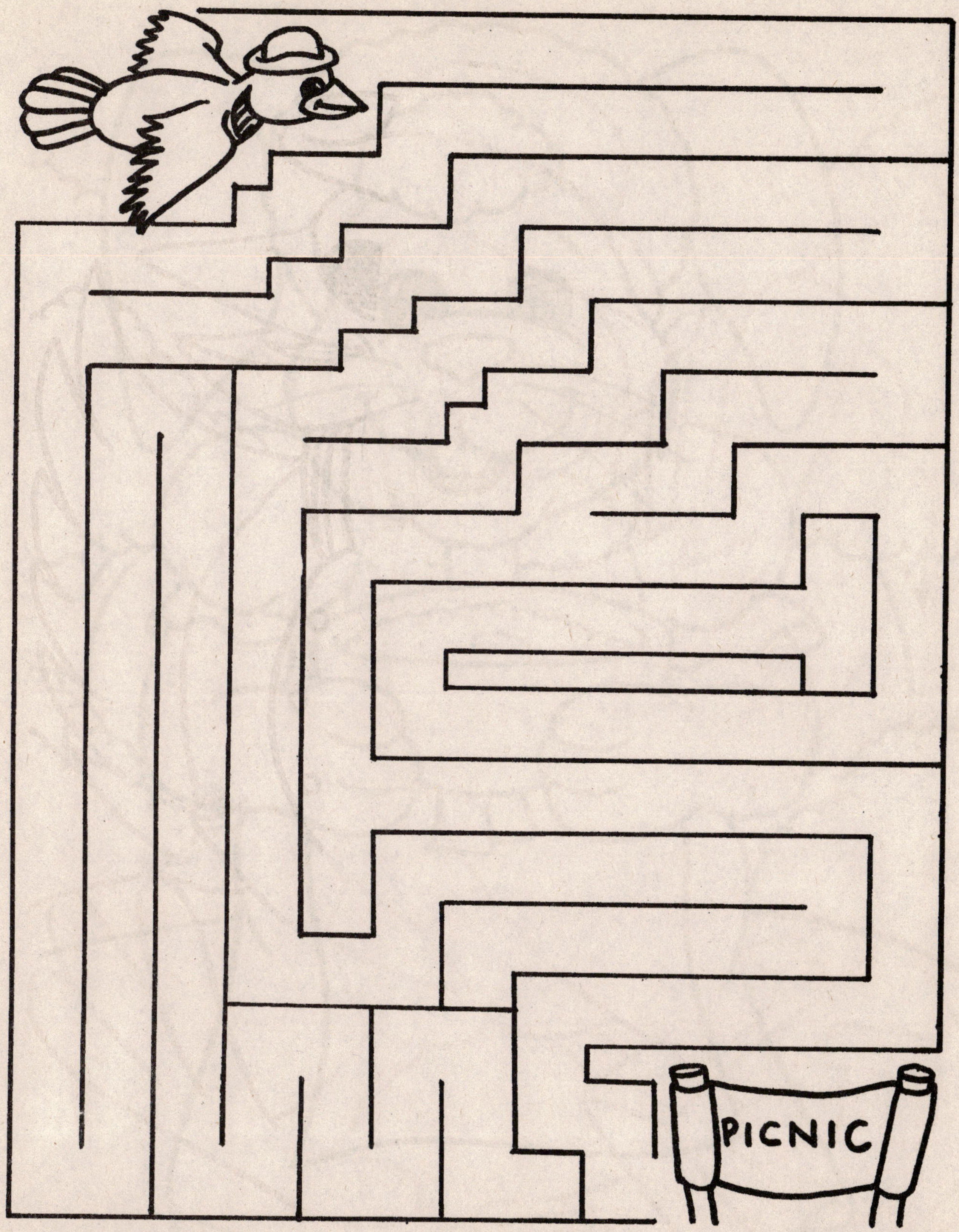

HELP ROBIN FIND HIS WAY TO THE PICNIC.

MRS. EASTER BUNNY BROUGHT EGG SALAD MADE FROM LEFTOVER EASTER EGGS.

CONNECT THE DOTS

PERCY AND PENELOPE PORCUPINE
SWEEP THE PICNIC AREA.

COLOR BY NUMBER

1. RED 2. ORANGE 3. YELLOW 4. GREEN 5. BLUE
6. PURPLE 7. BROWN

RICKY RACCOON BROUGHT A WATERMELON.

CONNECT THE DOTS

THE GEESE FLEW IN JUST IN TIME FOR THE PICNIC.

HOW MANY GEESE ARE IN THE FLOCK?

DIGBY DUCK WENT SWIMMING.

FILL IN THE MISSING LETTERS TO SPELL THE NAMES OF THE ANIMALS.

BILLY BEAR WOKE UP FROM HIS NAP
JUST IN TIME FOR THE PICNIC.

DRAW THE HANDS ON THE CLOCK TO SHOW WHAT TIME YOU WAKE UP.

ALL THE CHILDREN HUNTED BERRIES.

COLOR THE TEN BERRIES RED.

EXCEPT FOR SIMON SQUIRREL, WHO HUNTED NUTS INSTEAD.

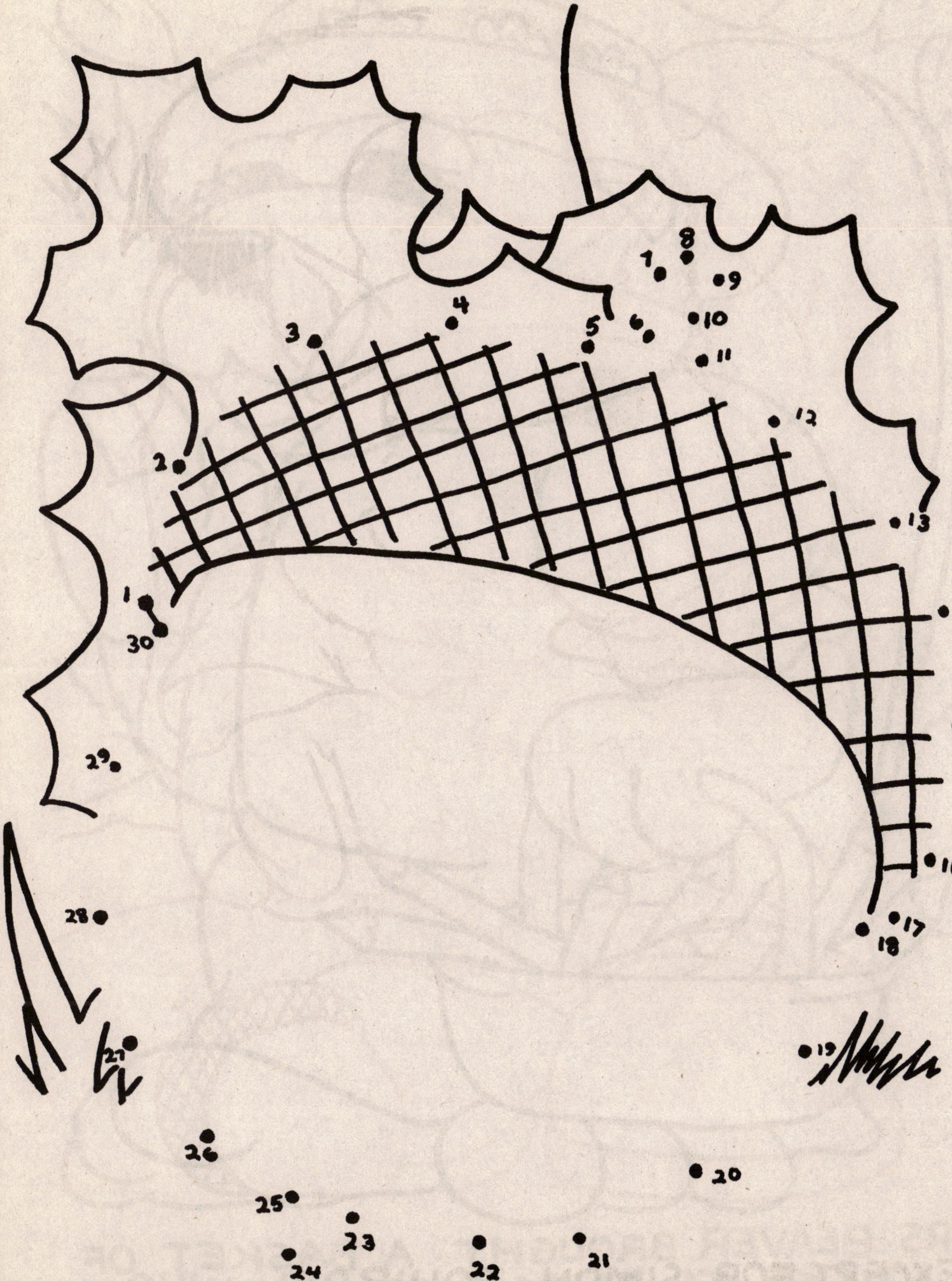

CONNECT THE DOTS.

MRS. BEAVER BROUGHT A BASKET OF STICKS TO SNACK ON.

FILL THIS BASKET WITH YOUR FAVORITE
PICNIC FOODS.

MR. ELEPHANT COOKED THE FOOD.

FILL IN THE NAMES OF THE ANIMALS TO SOLVE THE PUZZLE.

THE CROW MADE CORN ON THE COB.

THE SCARECROW DIDN'T SEEM TO MIND.
DRAW THE FACE ON THE SCARECROW.

MR. HORSE BROUGHT FRESH CARROTS FROM HIS GARDEN.

COLOR BY NUMBER

1. RED 2. ORANGE 3. YELLOW 4. GREEN 5. BLUE
6. PURPLE 7. BROWN

THE FROG KEPT THE BUGS AWAY.

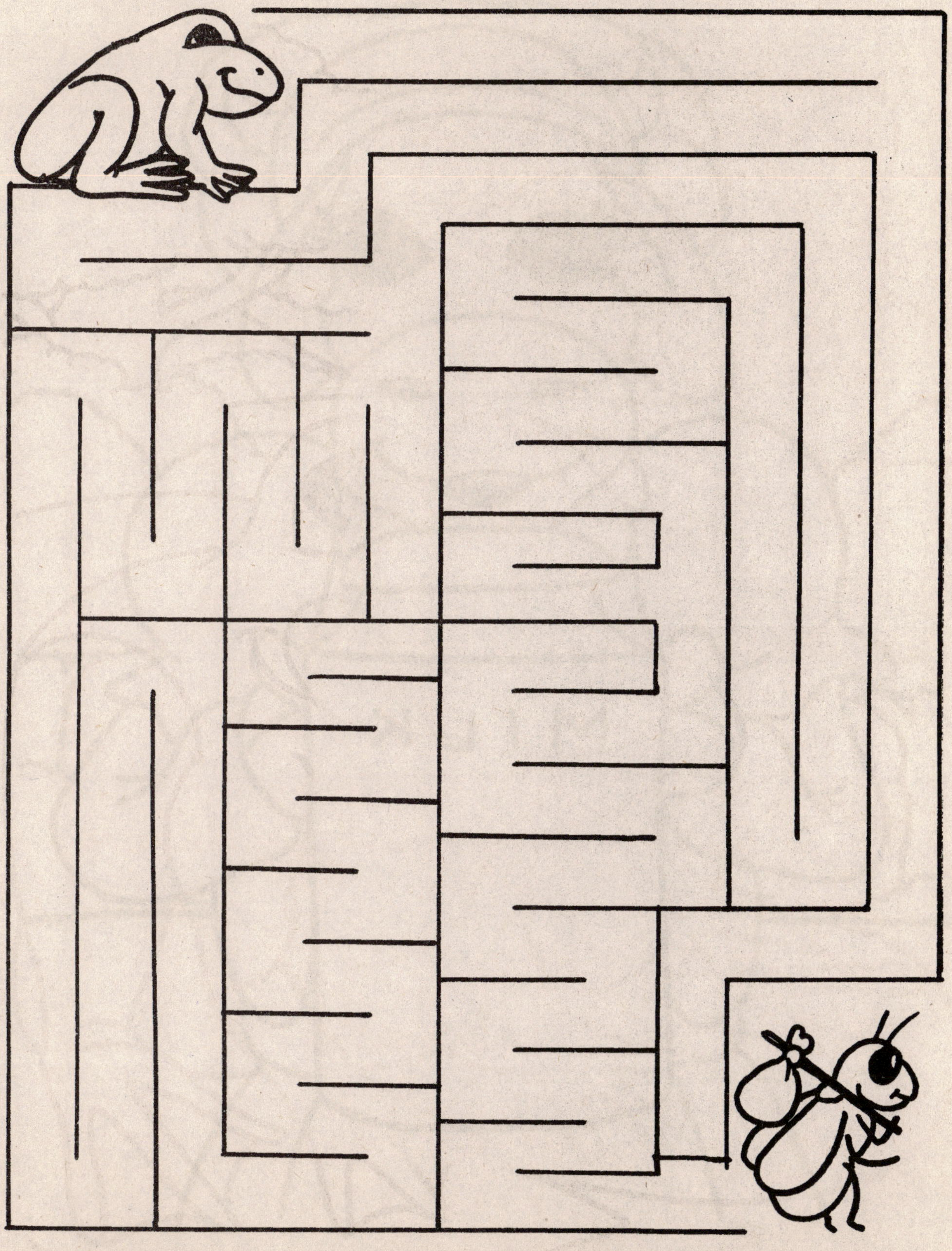

HELP THE FROG FIND THE FLY.

CLEMENTINE COW BROUGHT PLENTY OF MILK.

DAPHNE DOG PICKED BEAUTIFUL
SPRING FLOWERS FOR THE TABLES.

HOW MANY SPRING FLOWERS ARE IN THIS PICTURE?

THE MICE PLAYED HIDE AND GO SEEK
IN THE SWISS CHEESE.

THEY ATE A LITTLE, TOO.

COLOR BY NUMBER

1. PINK 2. BROWN 3. YELLOW 4. BLACK 5. ORANGE

MARTY ATE TOO MUCH AND GOT STUCK.

HELP THE MOUSE FIND HIS WAY THROUGH THE SWISS CHEESE.
ENTER
FINISH

THE LITTLE KITTENS DRINK FROM A SAUCER OF MILK.

COLOR THE PATCHES ON THE QUILT TO SEE THE SECRET MESSAGE.

1 YELLOW 2 BLUE 3 RED 4 BLACK

AFTER THEY ATE, THE ANIMALS ALL PLAYED GAMES.

CONNECT THE DOTS

BRANDON BUNNY PLAYED BASEBALL.

COLOR ALL THE SCOREBOARD LIGHTS WITH A DOT BLACK TO SEE WHAT BRANDON HIT.

PETER PIG WON THE PIE EATING CONTEST.

HOW MANY PIES DID PETER EAT?

PERCY PORCUPINE PLAYED VOLLEY-
BALL VERY CAREFULLY.

B _ _ L _ O _

H _ R _ E _ H _ E S

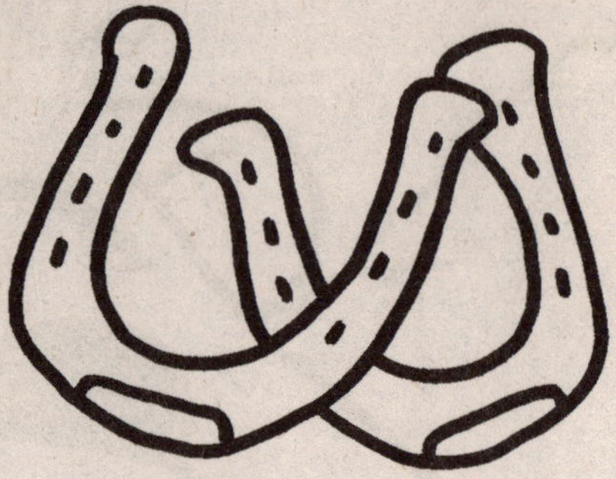

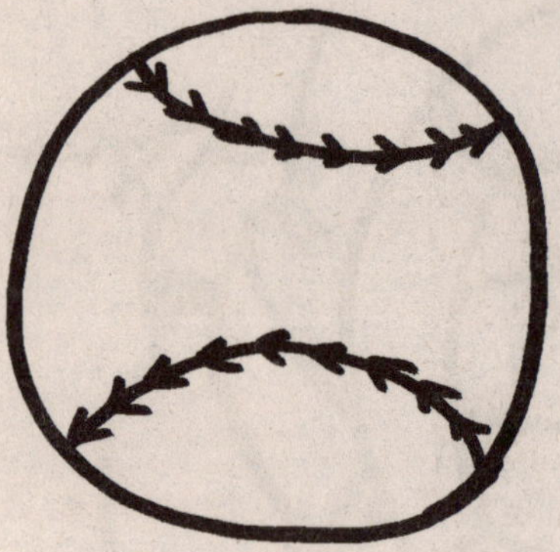

B _ S _ B _ _ L

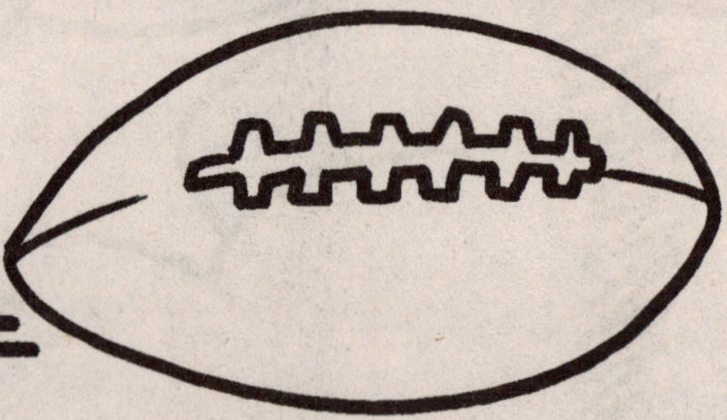

F _ O _ B _ _ L

V _ L L _ Y _ A _ _

FILL IN THE BLANKS!

THE FROGS WON THE LEAPFROG RELAY... AGAIN!

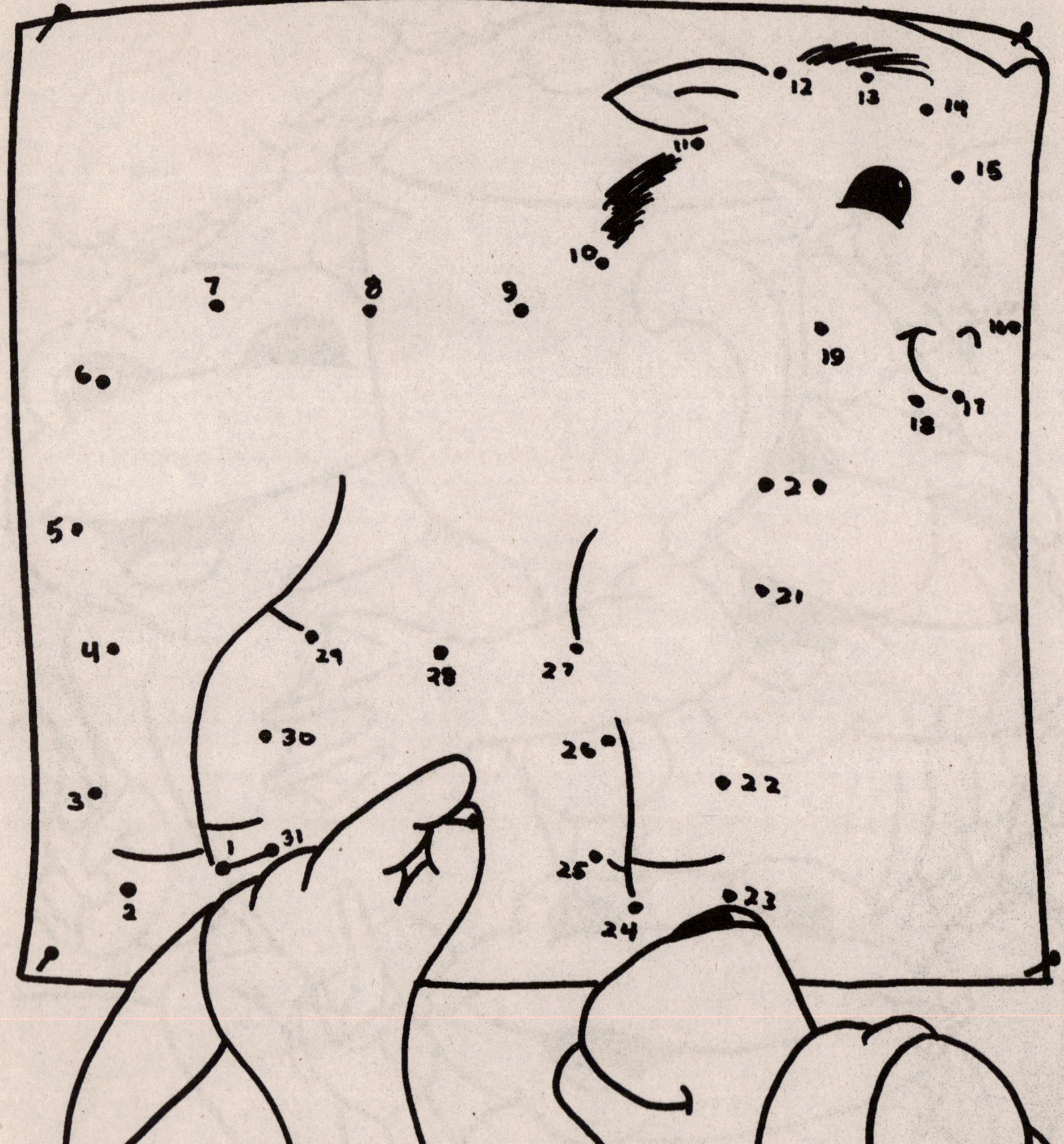

CONNECT THE DOTS.

LITTLE JUMBO WON THE PEANUT SCRAMBLE.

ALL THE LITTLE ONES HUNTED EGGS.

FIND THE 10 EGG SHAPES IN THIS PICTURE.

THE BUNNY BROTHERS WON THE SACK RACE

EVERYONE WAS SURPRISED WHEN
ONE OF OLLIE OTTER'S EGGS HATCHED.

COLOR BY NUMBER

1.RED 2.ORANGE 3.YELLOW 4.GREEN 5.BLUE 6.BROWN 7.PURPLE

CONNECT THE DOTS TO SEE THEIR TROPHY.

ROXY RACCOON LED THE NATURE WALK.

MATCH THE TRACK TO THE ANIMAL.

COLOR BY MATH ADD OR SUBTRACT THE PROBLEMS TO FIND THE COLOR NUMBERS 1. RED 2. ORANGE 3. YELLOW 4. GREEN 5. BLUE 6. PURPLE 7. BROWN

NO ONE WANTED TO RACE AGAINST
HARRY HARE IN THE RUNNING RACE.

"WHAT'S THE MATTER, ARE YOU ALL CHICKEN?," HARRY ASKED.

MRS. HENN WAS NOT AMUSED.

WHICH MRS. HENN IS DIFFERENT?

SLOWLY TIMMY TURTLE CRAWLED
TO THE STARTING LINE.

DRAW SNEAKERS ON TIMMY TURTLE.

HARRY FELL OVER WITH LAUGHTER.

MR. OWL STARTED THE RACE. "ON YOUR MARK, GET SET, GO." HE WAVED HIS FLAG AND THE RACE WAS ON.

TIMMY STARTED OFF RIGHT AWAY, HARRY WAS STILL LAUGHING.

TIMMY KEPT GOING. HARRY STOPPED AND ATE A PIECE OF WATERMELON.

HELP TIMMY FIND HIS WAY TO THE FINISH LINE.

TIMMY KEPT GOING. HARRY HAD A GLASS OF LEMONADE.

THEN HARRY LOOKED AND REALIZED THAT TIMMY WAS VERY CLOSE TO THE FINISH LINE.

HE RAN AS FAST AS HE COULD. TIMMY KEPT GOING.

COLOR BY NUMBER

1.RED 2.ORANGE 3.YELLOW 4.GREEN 5.BLUE
6.PURPLE 7.BROWN

TIMMY WAS THE BIG WINNER.

HARRY LEARNED HIS LESSON. HE WOULD TRY HARDER NEXT YEAR AND HE WOULDN'T BRAG SO MUCH.

THE BIG DAY WAS ALMOST OVER AND EVERY-
BODY HELPED TO CLEAN UP.

Some more springtime fun!

2 DANCING CHICKS!

WHERE ARE THE EGGS?

BUNNY PUPPET

BROWN HEN

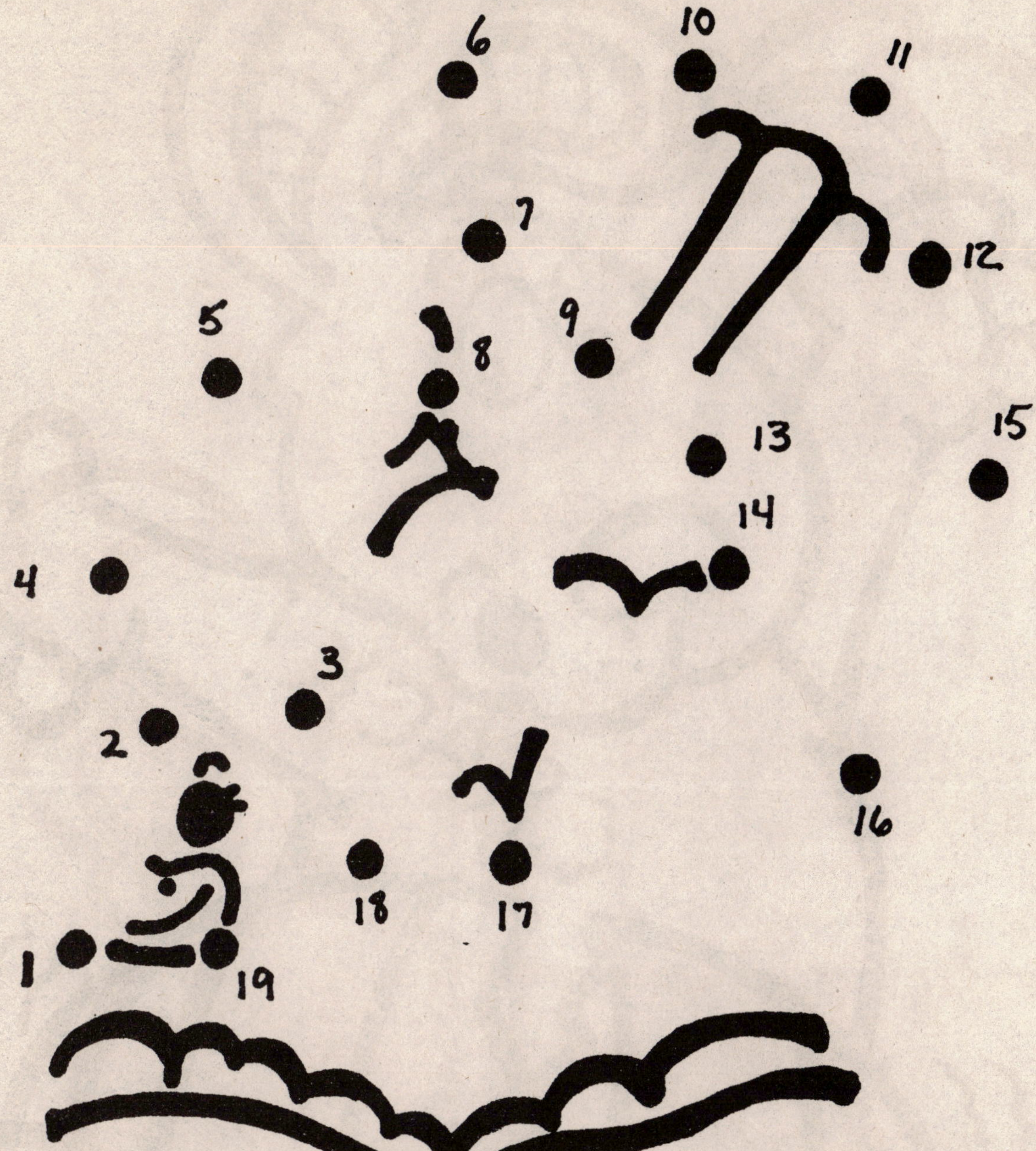

EASTER BIRD

OH NO!!

NEW DRESS

DAFFODILS

FIND THE FLOWERS

LOOK! IT'S A CHICK!

I LOVE BUNNY!

COLOR THE CHOCOLATE BUNNY BROWN

COUNT THE JELLYBEANS AND COLOR THEM DIFFERENT COLORS!

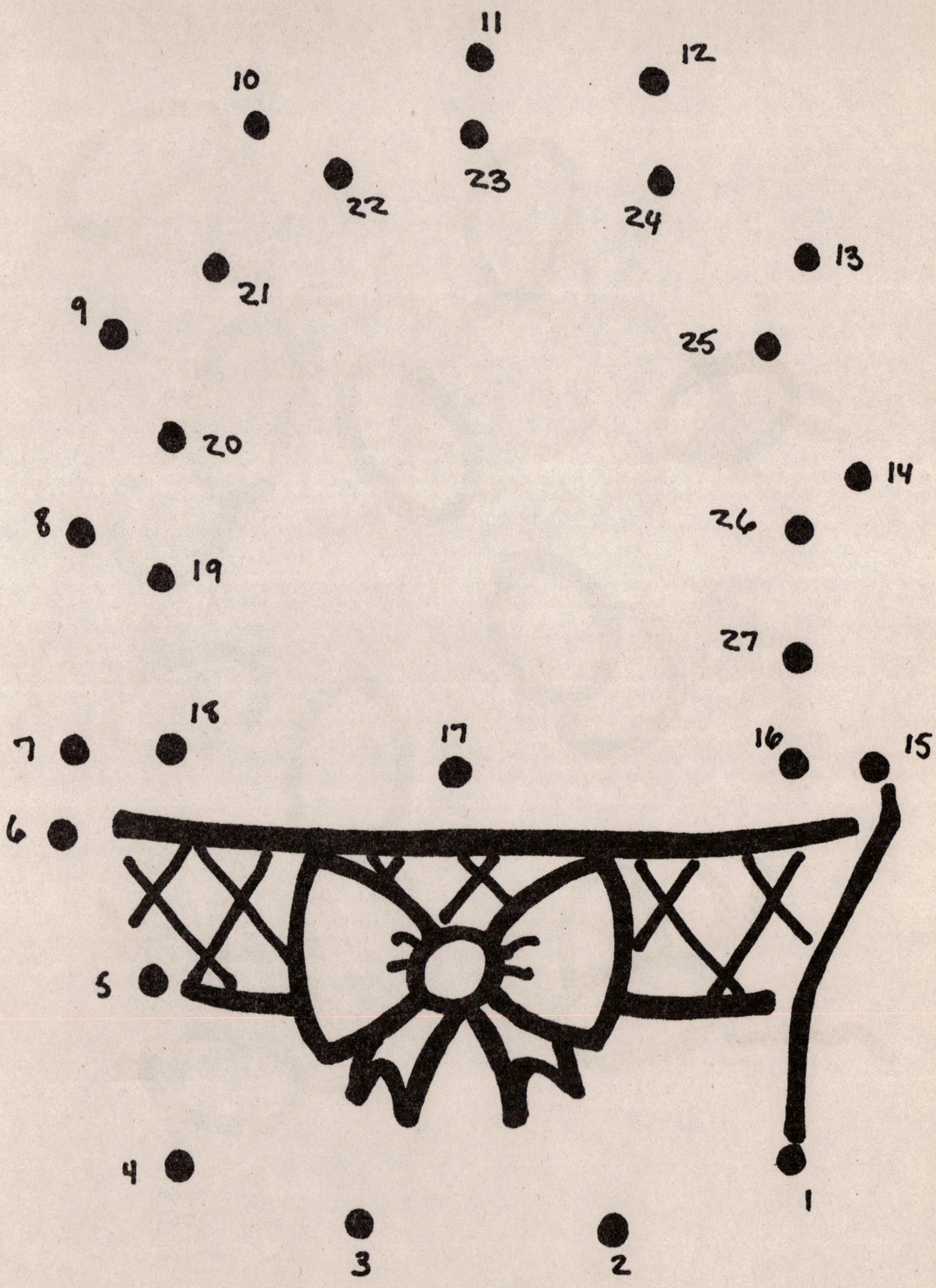

EASTER SURPRISE

TAKING A REST

QUACK QUACK

READY FOR BED

SPRINGTIME